Zoo Animals

POLAR BEARS AT THE ZOO

By Finn Ward

Gareth Stevens Publishing

Please visit our website, www.garethstevens.com. For a free color catalog of all our high-quality books, call toll free 1-800-542-2595 or fax 1-877-542-2596.

Library of Congress Cataloging-in-Publication Data

Ward, Finn.
Polar bears at the zoo / Finn Ward.
pages cm. — (Zoo animals)
Includes index.
ISBN 978-1-4824-2609-0 (pbk.)
ISBN 978-1-4824-2610-6 (6 pack)
ISBN 978-1-4824-2611-3 (library binding)
1. Polar bear—Juvenile literature. 2. Zoo animals—Juvenile literature. I. Title.
QL737.C27W367 2016
599.786—dc23
2015002599

First Edition

Published in 2016 by
Gareth Stevens Publishing
111 East 14th Street, Suite 349
New York, NY 10003

Editor: Ryan Nagelhout
Designer: Katelyn E. Reynolds

Photo credits: Cover, p. 1 Sean Gallup/Getty Images; p. 5 Richard Fellinger/Picture Press/Getty Images; p. 7 Rozhkova Irina/Shutterstock.com; pp. 9, 24 (fur) Sylvie Bouchard/Shutterstock.com; p. 11 Fotokon/Shutterstock.com; p. 13 Johann Helgason/Shutterstock.com; p. 15 Zhiltsov Alexandr/Shutterstock.com; pp. 17, 24 (carrot) Lindsay Dean/Shutterstock.com; p. 19 Igor Kovalchuk/Shutterstock.com; p. 21 olga_gl/Shutterstock.com; p. 23 andamanec/Shutterstock.com.

Printed in the United States of America

CPSIA compliance information: Batch #CS15GS: For further information contact Gareth Stevens, New York, New York at 1-800-542-2595.

Contents

Polar bears love the zoo!

Zoos keep them safe.

They have lots of fur.
It is white.

Polar bears are good swimmers.

They eat lots of food.

They eat lots of fish
in zoos.

They also eat carrots!

Baby polar bears
love to play.

Some play on rocks.

Others like to swim!

Words to Know

carrot

fur

Index